MORLEY LIBRARY
184 PHELPS STREET
PAINESVILLE, OHIO 44077
(440) 352-3383

Witches
and
Witchcraft

SECRETS OF THE SUPERNATURAL

Witches
and
Witchcraft

REBECCA STEFOFF

Marshall Cavendish
Benchmark
New York

Marshall Cavendish Benchmark
99 White Plains Road
Tarrytown, New York 10591-9001
www.marshallcavendish.us

Library of Congress Cataloging-in-Publication Data
Stefoff, Rebecca
Witches and witchcraft / by Rebecca Stefoff.
p. cm. — (Secrets of the supernatural)
Summary: "A critical exploration of witches and witchcraft" —Provided by publisher.
Includes bibliographical references and index.
ISBN-13: 978-0-7614-2637-0
1. Witches—Juvenile literature. 2. Witchcraft—Juvenile literature. I. Title.
BF1566.S7716 2007
133.4′3—dc22
2007013304

Editor: Joyce Stanton
Publisher: Michelle Bisson
Art Director: Anahid Hamparian
Series Designer: Anne Scatto / PIXEL PRESS

Images provided by Rose Corbett Gordon, Art Editor, Mystic, CT, from the following sources:
Cover: Réunion des Musées Nationaux/Art Resource, NY; *back cover:* Charles Walker/Topfoto/The Image
Works; *pages 1, 26, 52:* Charles Walker/Topfoto/The Image Works; *pages 2, 18, 28, 37, 40, 56:* Mary Evans
Picture Library/The Image Works; *pages 6, 21, 45:* Erich Lessing/Art Resource, NY; *page 8:* Private Collection,/
Bridgeman Art Library; *page 9:* The Art Archive; *page 11:* The Art Archive/Museo del Prado Madrid/Dagli Orti;
pages 12, 30: Réunion des Musées Nationaux/Art Resource, NY; *page 13:* Rebecca McEntee/Corbis Sygma;
page 15: Norbert von der Groeben/The Image Works; *page 16:* Giraudon/Art Resource, NY; *pages 20, 22, 55:*
The Art Archive/Culver Pictures; *page 24:* Richard T. Nowitz/Corbis; *page 29:* Gilles Mermet/Art Resource,
NY; *page 33:* Francis G. Mayer/Corbis; *page 34:* Gift of Frances Dworecki and children Roman Dworecki, Maria
Arnett and Harvey Arnett in memory of Sam Dworecki, to The Jewish Museum, New York/Photo by Richard
Goodbody, Inc./Art Resource, NY; *page 36:* Bildarchiv Preussischer Kulturbesitz/Art Resource, NY; *page 42:*
Bettmann/Corbis; *page 43:* Ann Ronan Picture Library, London/HIP/Art Resource, NY; *page 47:* Hulton
Archive/Getty Images; *page 50:* Collection of the New-York Historical Society/Bridgeman Art Library; *page 54:*
Peabody Essex Museum, Salem, Massachusetts/Bridgeman Art Library; *page 58:* The Art Archive/ Dagli Orti
(A); *page 60:* Floris Leeuwenberg/The Cover Story/Corbis; *page 63:* Blue Lantern Studio/Corbis; *page 66:*
Scott Olson/Getty Images; *page 67:* AP Photo/Debra Reid; *page 68:* Robert Huberman/SuperStock; *pages 70
& 77:* Snark/Art Resource, NY.

Printed in Malaysia

1   3   5   6   4   2

FRONT COVER: A witch, attended by her familiars
BACK COVER: An inscription on a tombstone records the fate of one
  Mary Parker, accused of witchcraft.
HALF TITLE: A mask once used in witchcraft rituals
TITLE PAGE: The devil leads his followers on a wild ride.

Contents

The officers of the Inquisition, an arm of the Roman Catholic Church, were powerful and feared. They collected accusations and confessions in the trials of men and women suspected of being witches.

Is It True?

"Many hundred thousand times good night, my daughter Veronica so dear to my heart," wrote Johannes Junius as he began a letter to his daughter. It took Junius many days to complete the letter because, as he told Veronica, his hands were badly mangled. They had been damaged during the torture.

Johannes Junius had the bad luck to live in the German principality of Bamberg in the early part of the seventeenth century. Bamberg was in the grip of a witch-hunting frenzy that lasted for years. Local judges, and many ordinary townsfolk as well, were consumed with the quest to find witches and punish them for the sin of witchcraft. So enthusiastically did they take up this mission that in 1627, Prince-Bishop Johann Georg II, the authority over Bamberg's political and religious life, had a special prison built for the purpose. It was called the hexenhaus *(witch house).*

The Bamberg hexenhaus *could hold thirty or more accused witches. It was equipped with cells, a room for guards, several rooms where prisoners were interrogated, a chapel, and a torture chamber that was built over a stream. Johannes Junius was unfortunate enough to become well acquainted with this sinister chamber.*

Junius's ordeal began on June 28, 1628. He was taken to the hexen-

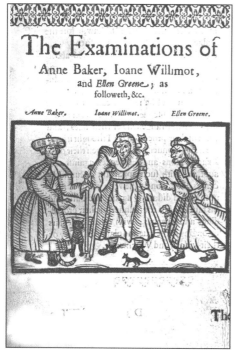

The Examinations of

'Anne Baker, Ioane Willimot, and *Ellen Greene*; as followeth, &c.

Anne Baker.   *Ioane Willimot.*   *Ellen Greene.*

The confessions of accused witches made popular reading in books and pamphlets.

haus *after a local man named Dr. Georg Adam Haan, who was being investigated as a witch, accused Junius of being one also. By that time the witch trials had been going on in Bamberg for several decades. Hundreds of people had been executed. Junius knew that the accusation was a desperately serious matter. He was a mayor of Bamberg, but his status wouldn't protect him. After all, it hadn't protected his wife. One year earlier she had been seized, tried, and killed as a witch.*

On entering the hexenhaus *Junius must have felt his spirits shrivel with terror. No one had ever been released from that place. But he firmly denied the charge of witchcraft. The questioners left him to think things over for two days. Then they approached him again and urged him to confess to being a witch. When he denied it a second time, the torture began. One of the torments inflicted on Junius was the strappado. In this cruel act, the victim's arms are tied behind him. The torturer then pulls him up by his tied hands to a height above the floor, then lets him drop. The plunge wrenches the victim's entire body and usually dislocates or breaks his shoulders.*

"I thought heaven and earth were at an end," Junius wrote to Veronica. "Eight times did they draw me up and let me fall again, so that I suffered horrible agony." Yet the official records of Junius's interrogation say that he experienced no pain under torture. This was a sure sign of a witch, because witches were supposed to be protected from pain by their unholy pact with the devil. Either the scribe who wrote the account

of Junius's torture did not know the truth about it, or he deliberately recorded a version that fit the interrogators' ideas of how a witch was expected to behave, not what really happened.

Someone else in the hexenhaus, however, was aware of Junius's suffering. Junius told Veronica that as his guard was leading him back to his cell after a session of questioning, the man said to him, "Sir, I beg you, for God's sake confess something, whether it be true or not. Invent something, for you cannot bear the torture which you shall suffer; and even if you bear it all, you still shall not escape, not even if you were a count, but one torture will follow another until you say you are a witch. Not before that will they let you go, as you may see by their trials, for one is just like another."

Junius asked for time to think it over. The thought of saying that he had turned his back on God and become a witch was dreadful, but the prospect of further torture was unbearable. Finally he decided to invent a confession. He told a story of having met a girl who turned into a goat and forced him to swear allegiance to the devil. Yes, he admitted, that had made him a witch.

An English pamphlet from 1589 records the hanging of three witches in the town of Chelmsford.

The confession wasn't enough. Wasn't it true, Junius's questioners demanded, that he had danced with other witches? Junius had heard such things read aloud from confessions in earlier witchcraft cases in Bamberg, so he agreed. The questioners then insisted that he name the other witches. When he said that he hadn't recognized any of them, the questioners threatened

him with renewed torture. Then they named the streets of Bamberg, one after another, and the miserable Junius said that he had recognized people from some of the streets at the witches' dance. Under the threat of torture, he accused other citizens of Bamberg, just as Haan had accused him.

It still wasn't enough. The questioners wanted to know exactly what evil acts Junius had performed as a witch. Finally, after he had made up some things to tell them, they were finished with him. He endured several weeks of imprisonment, during which he managed to write the letter to Veronica. He told her, "Now dear child, here you have all my confession and [the record of] my trial, for which I must die. And they are sheer lies and inventions, so help me God." He then advised Veronica to leave Bamberg for a time for her own safety, "until it becomes clear what turn things will take." He also told her to keep the letter safely hidden and to give a little money to the man who was to smuggle it to her. The letter ends, "Good night, for your father Johannes Junius will never see you again."

Junius was put to death as a witch on August 6, 1628. Some accounts of the case say that the judges showed Junius a final favor, perhaps because of his status or because he had made no public attempt to recant, or take back, his confession. They allowed him to be beheaded with a sword, rather than burned alive.

When you think of witches, do you picture someone like Veronica's father—a middle-aged, well-known civic official, deeply attached to his daughter and horrifically unlucky? Or is your idea of a witch a cackling old hag with a cloak and a pointed hat, casting curses as she flies through the night sky on her broomstick? Or is it a kindly healer, skilled in brewing herbal potions? Maybe the image that comes to your mind is something more modern—a sassy teenager or a suburban housewife who just happens to have some very special, mischief-making powers. The word *witch* has meant all of these, and much more.

What Is a Witch?

Images of witches and their deeds come to us from folklore around the world, from historical accounts of witch trials, and from traditional fairy tales and modern media. The witches in these images fit no simple pattern. They may be old or young, male or female, good or bad, learned scholars or unschooled peasants. But all witches have one thing in common: they can use magic.

What is magic? Gerald B. Gardner, whose 1954 book, *Witchcraft Today,* inspired the modern witchcraft movement known as Wicca, called it "the art of getting results." Magic is the use of special power or knowledge to affect the physical world. Like all forms of magic, witchcraft is based on the belief that there are ways to influence situations that go beyond ordinary experience and the known laws of science and the

A wrinkled cackling old crone is probably our most typical image of a witch.

physical world. A witch may cause events to happen, or shift the balance of chance and fate. (Some modern witches use the word *magick* when talking about witchcraft, to separate it from stage magic, the skilled but nonsupernatural tricks performed by professional magicians and illusionists.)

Stories about witches suggest that they can acquire their ability to perform magic in various ways. A witch may be born with the ability, or gain it through study and practice, or receive it from a spirit, demon, or other nonhuman being. Whatever the source of their power, witches can work their will upon the world, in large ways or in small ones.

Magic and Reality

Who wouldn't want to possess a secret power to smooth life's rough path? Who hasn't dreamed of being able to make annoyances disappear, to turn bad luck into good—or even, in our darker

moments, to strike back at someone who has hurt us?

Witches have been thought to use their power in a wide variety of ways: healing, predicting or foreseeing the future, finding out secrets, spoiling food and making animals sick,

Dutch painter Frans Hals depicted Crazy Barbara, a real-life woman whom some called a witch. Others said she was merely insane.

casting spells to bring good fortune (or bad fortune, if the spell is a curse), communicating with invisible spirits, changing their shapes to those of animals, flying, and even causing sickness or death. Have any witches ever actually *done* these things? Is witchcraft real?

Countless people throughout history have believed that witchcraft is very real. The fate of Johannes Junius shows that whole communities and cultures have taken extreme actions based on their witchcraft beliefs. Don't think, though, that witches and witchcraft are found only in dusty history books or old fairy tales.

The five-pointed star, or pentagram, long associated with magic, is a Wiccan symbol.

Witchcraft is in the news. Wiccans today, for example, have won some degree of legal recognition that their beliefs are a religion, but the subject remains controversial. When a Wiccan soldier was killed in Afghanistan in 2005, for example, his widow fought successfully for the right to have the pentagram—a Wiccan symbol associated with magic and witchcraft—displayed on his grave in a state military cemetery. She ran into opposition because other religions, including certain versions of Christianity, strongly oppose the mere idea of witchcraft.

Concerns about witchcraft extend to the popular fiction kids enjoy. In some communities, for example, school board meetings have turned into shouting matches about whether children should be allowed to read tales of the boy wizard Harry Potter. But fear of witchcraft goes far beyond the question of reading matter. In some countries, people are still being killed as witches, either executed by the state or dragged from their homes and murdered by frightened mobs. So witchcraft surely exists, in the form of a belief shared by many people and societies both past and present. Whether there is genuine substance to witchcraft—whether a witch really *is* different from the rest of us—is another matter.

"Extraordinary claims require extraordinary proof," the astronomer Carl Sagan once said. His statement has become a motto for skeptics, people who use reason and critical thinking to examine claims about the world. When confronted with a claim of something beyond the ordinary, a good critical thinker doesn't simply say that it can't be true. He or she asks to see the evidence, or invites people to think about what *kind* of evidence could prove the claim. A skeptic's goal is to get at the truth, whenever possible.

Witchcraft is supposed to produce effects in the physical world that are caused by the witch's will, not by natural processes or scientific principles. This puts witchcraft into the "extraordinary" category. If you choose to think critically about witches and witchcraft, you will find that one useful tool is the question, what is the evidence? As you read or hear witchcraft stories, ask yourself who is telling the story, and what motives he or she might have for telling it a certain way. Does the evidence seem reliable to you?

No one has ever produced solid proof of any of the spectacular feats credited to witches. You won't find genuine videos of a wizard turning someone into a toad, or of a witch riding on a broom. A modern witch would probably say that witchcraft is not about performing such stunts. It's about living in a certain way, acting in harmony with the forces of nature. Instead of turning people into toads, a witch might use magic for help in focusing thoughts or making decisions.

Is reading about magic and wizardry harmful to young people? Harry Potter's many fans don't think so.

In the pages that follow, you'll discover the many fascinating—and frightful—forms that witchcraft has taken around the world. You'll see how changing ideas about witchcraft led to witch hunts and trials, including America's famous Salem trials, and how beliefs about witches still affect people today. You'll find eerie tales of witches past, and you'll see what life is like for a typical modern teenage witch. Along the way, you may decide for yourself what you think about the mysterious, sometimes terrifying figure of the witch, whose hold on our imaginations is as strong today as it ever was.

Witches gather for an unholy meeting in this painting
by the Spanish artist Francisco Goya. One witch holds an
infant up to the devilish goat—some claimed that
witches practiced human sacrifice.

A World of Witchcraft

All magic was bad to the Azande people of central Africa. Their traditional beliefs said that anyone who had supernatural powers used those powers to harm others. Such people could destroy property, make accidents happen, and cause sickness or death. In the Azande worldview, there was no good magic, or "white magic," but there were two kinds of magic makers: witches and sorcerers.

Witches had powers and knowledge that ordinary people could never understand. The reasons for their magical acts were also beyond the ordinary, for witches were bizarre beings, driven by strange or supernatural urges and needs. Sorcery, on the other hand, was destructive magic performed by ordinary people. Sorcerers acted for bad but understandably human reasons, such as greed, desire, or revenge. Unlike witchcraft, sorcery was available to anyone who chose to use the necessary materials or spells. The Azande regarded both witches and sorcerers with fear and disgust, as "enemies of men," according to E. E. Evans-Pritchard, a scholar who studied Azande magical beliefs. Yet other cultures have held different views about witchcraft. In some, witches have been accepted, even respected.

Sorcerers, Necromancers, and Wizards

If you dip into the vast library of works about witchcraft and magic, you'll find that the vocabulary is often confusing. The same word can have many different meanings. *Sorcery* is a good example. The scholar who studied the Azande used it as a label for one of the two kinds of magic making they recognized. But other writers use *sorcery* to mean *witchcraft*, with no real difference between the two terms.

Sorcery has other meanings as well. It sometimes refers to "book" magic, the practices of learned people who have studied occult lore, as distinct from peasant or folk witchcraft. Sorcery may also describe black magic, or harmful witchcraft—the use of magical techniques for evil, destructive, or forbidden purposes. Finally,

some scholars who study the history of magic use *sorcery* for the broad body of beliefs about magic making around the world, limiting *witchcraft* to the period during which people like Johannes Junius were persecuted in Christian Europe. You could fill a book with the different definitions— and that's just for *sorcery*!

Wizards, or male magic makers, appear wise and good in some tales. Still, many men were hanged as witches.

Some particular kinds of magic making have their own names. Necromancers, for example, practice necromancy, the art of communicating with the spirits of the dead to gain knowledge from them. Shamans use their supernatural powers for healing. Seers, oracles, diviners, and prophets use them for seeing the future. Today, many people who follow some form of witchcraft call themselves Wiccans, Pagans, or Druids. All of these have been called witches at one time or another. And although most people think of witches as female, men have been witches, too, although a male witch might also be called a warlock or a wizard.

Witches' Powers

Witchcraft is a worldwide phenomenon. The idea of the witch is so widespread that some researchers think it may have been part of the belief system of our early Stone Age ancestors. As they spread across the world, so did the belief in witchcraft.

Certain ideas about witches appear over and over again in a wide variety of cultures and geographic locations. One of these near-universal ideas is that witches have servants or companions called familiars. Sometimes the familiar is a monster or magical being. Certain Bantu-speaking peoples in Africa, for example, describe witches' familiars as dwarflike creatures called *tokoloshe* or *tikoloshe*. Often the familiar is an animal, bird, or even an insect with which the witch can communicate. Many Chinese witches had foxes or dogs as familiars. Russian ones often had chickens, serpents, weasels, and mice. An African witch might have a leopard, a hyena, a red ant, or a baboon. In Central America, a witch's familiar could be a bat or a lizard.

European witches had bats, owls, ferrets, mice, toads, goats, rabbits, and dogs as familiars, but the most common familiar was the cat.

Harmless household pets, kept for companionship or for their services in getting rid of mice and rats, could easily be suspected of being familiars. That's why, even now, witches often appear in pictures and stories accompanied by cats. (Over time, black cats became especially associated in people's minds with harmful witches.)

What did a familiar do? It spied on people in the community and carried news to the witch. It also ran errands for the witch, collecting the materials needed for magical charms and potions. Such ingredients could range from medicinal herbs and flowers to items more sinister and repulsive. William Shakespeare's play *Macbeth*, which features three witches who forecast the future and brew potions, contains a gruesome list of ingredients: "Eye of newt, and toe of frog/Wool of bat, and tongue of dog." Their hellish brew also contains a dragon's scale, a wolf's tooth, a baboon's blood, the mummy of a witch, and some human remains, including "finger of birth-strangled babe." Not every witch's recipe was as fanciful as the one

Shakespeare invented, but his list touches on one widely shared belief—that witches used human parts in their rituals. (They were also thought to be cannibals who ate human flesh.)

A witch's familiar could be more than a servant or an

An American Halloween postcard from 1920 features a witch with three common accessories: a pointed hat, a broomstick, and a black cat.

errand runner. Sometimes familiars were thought to teach the witches their magical practices, or even to give them orders. In these cases, the witch was the servant of the familiar.

Another common idea about witches is that they could travel by means unknown to ordinary people, usually by flying. In Europe witches were at first thought to fly by riding upon monstrous beasts, or spirits. They would fly by night and gather at secret meeting places. The first reference to this "witches' ride" appeared around 900 CE* in a collection of church laws called the Canon Episcopi. Centuries later, the idea took hold that witches rode broomsticks. In central Africa witches also flew through the night on household tools—the large, flat baskets that people used for sifting grain. Sometimes a witch's method of travel was more mysterious. In the American Southwest, a witch might simply appear somewhere suddenly and unexpectedly, having covered an impossible distance in a short time.

The three witches of *Macbeth* utter a fateful prediction that dooms a king.

Shape-shifting is another power often associated with witchcraft. Witches were believed to be able to turn into wolves, cats, foxes, coyotes, and other creatures. Sometimes witches also transformed

---

*A variety of systems of dating have been used by different cultures throughout history. Many historians now prefer to use BCE (Before Common Era) and CE (Common Era) instead of BC (Before Christ) and AD (Anno Domini), out of respect for the diversity of the world's peoples.

The witches in this French illustration don't need broomsticks—their familiars carry them through the sky. One familiar is an owl, considered spooky by some because it flies by night.

themselves while remaining in human form. They might take on the likeness of another person or change their own appearance to look younger or more beautiful. This type of shape-shifting was usually done to deceive or entrap victims.

If witches were so powerful, how could people protect themselves? One way was to avoid making a witch angry. Folktales from many cultures tell of people who were rude to someone—perhaps refusing to share food with a wandering man, or speaking harshly to an old woman on the road—only to discover to their dismay that the offended person was a witch who repaid the rudeness with a curse. Such tales suggest that it is wise to be polite and generous to strangers. A few modern social scientists have even suggested that witchcraft belief served a useful purpose by encouraging good behavior.

Strangely enough, the best shield against witchcraft was sometimes . . . witchcraft. To fight off any harmful magic that might be turned against them, people relied on protective magic: spells or amulets (charms). This type of supernatural protection is called apotropaic magic by scholars, and it is found everywhere that witchcraft occurs. People could perform apotropaic magic for themselves, using words and ingredients known to all through folklore, or they could seek the professional aid of a good witch—or at least a neutral one.

The "evil eye" is an example of the harm a witch could do and the ways people protected themselves from it. Witches were often accused of bewitching people or animals, causing them to fall ill or die, just by staring at them. This was called fascination or the evil eye. In the sixteenth century, a student of witchcraft named William Perkins described how a witch could send evil supernatural spirits from his or her eyes:

> *It is an old received opinion, that in malicious and ill-disposed persons, there proceed out of the eye with the beams noisome and malignant spirits, which infect the air, and do poison or kill not only them with whom they are daily conversant, but others also whose company they frequent, of what age, strength, or complexion so ever they be.*

People with unusual eyes—perhaps cross-eyed, or squinting, or of two different colors—were at risk of being considered witches. Bright green or blue eyes were highly suspicious. Any prolonged stare or angry glare could bring an accusation of witchcraft.

For protection from the evil eye, people wore amulets, and they put them on their children and livestock, too. An amulet might be an inscribed ring, a red ribbon, or a piece of coral. Those who could not obtain or afford such charms could use cords that they had tied in knots while chanting a protective spell, or necklaces

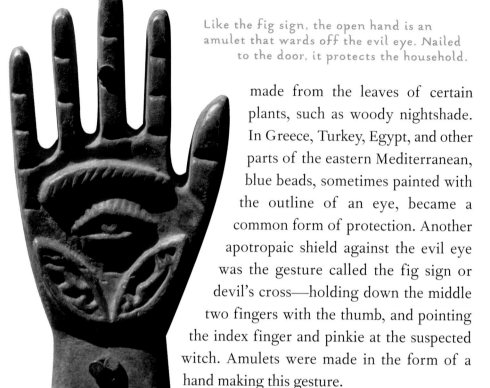

Like the fig sign, the open hand is an amulet that wards off the evil eye. Nailed to the door, it protects the household.

made from the leaves of certain plants, such as woody nightshade. In Greece, Turkey, Egypt, and other parts of the eastern Mediterranean, blue beads, sometimes painted with the outline of an eye, became a common form of protection. Another apotropaic shield against the evil eye was the gesture called the fig sign or devil's cross—holding down the middle two fingers with the thumb, and pointing the index finger and pinkie at the suspected witch. Amulets were made in the form of a hand making this gesture.

Witches of the Ancient World

Some of the oldest written records of witchcraft come from the Middle Eastern land of Mesopotamia, now known as Iraq. Starting around six thousand years ago, a series of civilizations rose and flourished in that region: Sumerian, Akkadian, Assyrian, Babylonian. All of these ancient societies had magical beliefs, including the belief that witches or sorcerers could directly harness supernatural powers.

Magic was neither black nor white in Mesopotamia. The same witchcraft techniques—spells, rituals, charms—could be used for either good or evil. The difference lay in the intention of the sorcerer. A witch using magic to do harm did so in secret, but people who used magic in harmless ways acted openly.

If attacked by witchcraft, a person could perform a ritual to block the attack and turn it back against the witch who had launched it. The details of such a ritual have been preserved in an ancient Mesopotamian text called *Maqlû,* which means "burning." It tells how the victim makes an image of the witch, then performs a protective ritual that ends with the destruction of the image. The victim utters this spell:

> *My witch and my sorceress is sitting in the shadow behind*
> *a brick pile.*
> *She is sitting there, practicing witchcraft against me,*
> *fashioning figurines of me.*
> *I am going to dispatch against you thyme and sesame,*
> *I will scatter your sorceries, will stuff your words back into*
> *your mouth!*
> *May the witchcraft you performed be aimed at yourself,*
> *may the figurines you made represent yourself, may the*
> *water you drew be that of your own body!*
> *May your spell not close in on me, may your words not*
> *overcome me.*

This spell tells us that Mesopotamian sorcery shared key features with witchcraft from many other times and places. One feature is the use of herbs or plants. Another is the making of a small statue or figurine to represent the person against whom the magic is directed.

Witchcraft is mentioned in some collections of ancient Mesopotamian laws, but there is no evidence of any witchcraft trials—possibly because a charge of witchcraft could backfire against the accuser. Someone who accused another person of sorcery might have to undergo a physical ordeal to prove his or her own innocence. The accuser would be cast into a sacred river to sink or swim. Only the innocent could survive. An accuser who drowned was a witch.

The ancient Greeks and Romans believed in an array of gods, goddesses, and other semidivine and supernatural beings. One of these figures was Hecate, the dangerous, unpredictable goddess of the underworld, magic, and witchcraft. Hecate was sometimes portrayed as a threefold figure: a young girl, a mature woman, and an aged crone all at once. This image of the triple goddess became part of Western folklore and survives in some forms of Wicca today.

The witch lore of the Romans included beliefs and stories from all of Greece, western Asia, and Egypt as well as the Italian peninsula. Roman society had "official" magic makers who performed magical rituals and foretold the future on behalf of the state. Unofficial witches and sorcerers also plied their trade for clients. They cast spells, told fortunes, and prescribed both herbal and magical treatments for the sick. They also sold amulets, or protective charms, and talismans, which are charms to attract love or good fortune. At other times in the long history of Roman civilization, the authorities frowned on sorcery, forcing magic makers and their customers into some degree of secrecy.

Hecate, the Greek goddess of the underworld, is sometimes shown with the heads of three different women. Here she is animal-headed, like the deities of ancient Egypt.

The life and work of Lucius Apuleius offer a glimpse of Roman attitudes toward magic, in real life as well as in fiction. Apuleius, who lived in the second century CE, was born in the Roman province of Numidia, now the North African nation of Algeria. He traveled through the eastern part of the Roman Empire and developed a deep interest in religious and magical cults.

After living in Rome for a time, Apuleius returned to Africa and married a rich widow. Her relatives accused him of having bewitched her, using sorcery to gain her affections (and her fortune). Apuleius successfully defended himself from this charge, then spent the rest of his life studying and writing. His best-known work, a novel called *Metamorphoses* (also known as *The Golden Ass*), brims with witchcraft. It is the story of a young man who is magically turned into a donkey. In the course of his adventures, he meets others who have had encounters with enchantment and sorcery. One of them, a man named Thelyphron, had suffered a strange ordeal that involved savage witches *and* a learned magician. He recounts his experience in Book 2 of *Metamorphoses*.

When Thelyphron was a young student, with little money, he traveled through Thessaly, a wild region in northern Greece. In the town of Larissa he heard that a large reward was being offered to anyone who would stand guard over a corpse throughout the night.

Thelyphron asked about the reward and was told that the witches of Thessaly were notorious for attacking corpses. The witches bit off dead people's noses and the flesh from their faces for use in sorcerous spells. Guarding a corpse was no easy job, because the witches could enter the room in animal form and bewitch the guard. But Thelyphron volunteered for the job anyway—he needed the reward money.

He was taken to a house where he found a beautiful widow crying over the corpse of her dead husband. All too soon, Thelyphron was left alone with the corpse and a lamp. As he fought against sleep, he saw a weasel slip into the room through a hole in the door. The animal stared at Thelyphron. This made him horribly uneasy, because such behavior wasn't natural, but the weasel ran away when he shouted at it. Soon afterward, though, Thelyphron fell into a deep sleep. When he woke up in the morning, he rushed to the bed and looked at the corpse. To his relief, he saw that its face was unharmed.

After receiving his reward, Thelyphron decided to watch the burial procession pass through town. A large crowd had gathered when an old man ran up and interrupted the procession with a terrible accusation: the widow had poisoned her husband! The old man was the dead man's uncle and was convinced that he had been murdered. Soon the whole crowd was shouting, some taking the uncle's side, others supporting the widow. Then the uncle introduced Zachlas, an impressive-looking man with a white robe and a shaved head. Zachlas, said the uncle, was one of the greatest magicians of Egypt. He could bring the dead man back to life for a short while—just long enough for the man to tell how he had died.

The crowd watched in awe as Zachlas performed his ritual. The magician touched the mouth of the corpse with an herb and then prayed to the rising sun. In a few moments the corpse sat up. Groaning, the dead man said that his wife had poisoned him because she had fallen in love with another.

The dead man's revelations made the crowd more excited and confused than ever. Some of the bystanders called for the widow's death. Another group argued that the corpse should not be trusted. Its words could be a trick. The dead man then declared that he could prove his word by revealing something that no one else could possibly know. Turning, the dead man pointed straight at Thelyphron.

The corpse said that witches had come into the death chamber the night before, in the form of weasels and mice. They cast a sleeping spell on the guard, and then they called the dead man by name. But it happened that the dead man's name was the same as the guard's: Thelyphron. So the sleeping guard rose and answered the witches' call in place of the corpse. The witches gnawed away his fingers and ears and replaced them with wax—

As the dead man reached this point in his tale, Thelyphron the guard grabbed at his nose and ears. To his horror, they came off in his hands. They were only wax!

A beautiful woman, eerie animals, wicked witches, betrayal, poison, a talking corpse, and a wise magician—the tale of Thelyphron has many elements of a classic witch story. But Thelyphron was luckier than many unfortunate victims of witchcraft. He lived to tell his tale.

The Golden Ass is the story of a young man who is turned into a donkey because of his excessive interest in magic and witchcraft.

Condemned by the Inquisition, this man has been garroted, or strangled. Suspected witches were often executed in public, and their bodies were displayed as warnings of the fate of evildoers.

The Hammer and the Hunt

For a long time, witchcraft and religion existed side by side in the Western world, as they do in many countries today. A French peasant of the eighth century CE could go to church regularly and consider himself a good Christian, yet when he got sick he would make his way to the cottage of the local wise-woman, who cured with charms as well as herbal remedies. A tenth-century English girl would be doing nothing unusual if she gathered certain flowers, braided them into a necklace, and whispered the words of a spell to make someone fall in love with her.

But the Christian church never approved of magic. Although at first it often ignored or tolerated magical practices, in time its attitude hardened. Influenced by religious thinkers and judges called demonologists, the church became determined to stamp out the menace of magic.

Fear of witchcraft bubbled through all ranks of society, from rulers to peasants, in both Catholic and Protestant countries. Witch-hunters, church courts, and civic leaders took their inspiration from a harsh biblical statement: "Thou shalt not suffer a witch to live" (Exodus 22:18). The result was a wave of accusations, trials, and killings that reached their peak in the fifteenth through the seventeenth centuries. Some modern writers have called it the Great Witch Hunt.

A Deal with the Devil?

European witchcraft in the early centuries of Christianity was a mixture of folklore and witch stories, herbal medicine, and beliefs and practices carried over from earlier, pre-Christian times, such as hanging a piece of iron on a house as protection from a witch's curse. The church regarded witchcraft and magic as relics of paganism, the worship of many gods. Witchcraft belief was wrong not just because of its pagan connections, however, but also because, church officials said, it tricked people into thinking that they could control things that only God controls.

Church authorities disagreed about whether witchcraft was real. Some leading religious thinkers believed in the existence of magic. They considered it dangerous and evil, the work of the devil. Many others, however, took a different view. They said that the *desire* to do witchcraft was wicked, and the act of performing sorcery was a sin, but magic itself was nothing more than ignorant pagan superstition, because only God could perform miracles. This was the view of the tenth-century Canon Episcopi, which said that belief in witchcraft was false.

Under church law, it was illegal to perform acts of sorcery, but in practice the law was enforced very unevenly. The church occasionally took action when people were accused of *maleficium*, or harmful sorcery. Yet fortune-telling, spell casting, and amulet wearing continued as they had done since pagan times. Throughout the Middle Ages, into the fourteenth century, the clergy and the courts generally greeted accusations of witchcraft with skepticism. The church's official teaching was that witches did not exist.

Witchcraft became a more serious threat, however, after several centuries of religious conflicts within the Roman Catholic faith. Starting in the twelfth century, the church battled repeated outbreaks of heresy, religious beliefs that departed from the official teachings of the church. Several of these heresies, such as the Waldensian and Albigensian movements, attracted many followers and spread over large areas. They threatened the church's authority over religion.

A young man consults a fortune-teller. Officially forbidden by the church, fortune-telling and other supposedly magical practices were common in Europe through the Middle Ages and beyond.

An accused woman is questioned in prison. In the era of the European witch hunts, some people feared that witchcraft would undermine the social order.

To deal with heresy, the system of ecclesiastical, or church, courts grew larger and more powerful. Officers called inquisitors were charged with identifying heretics—people who believed heresies—so that they could be punished. The inquisitorial system allowed the court to investigate people based on rumors alone; no specific charges were needed. People suspected or accused of heresy were tried in secret proceedings, without legal help. Their interrogations often included torture. Although some accused heretics were later released, many were executed. One widely used method of execution was public burning.

The most troublesome heresies had been stamped out or contained by the end of the fourteenth century. By that time, however, witchcraft had become entangled with heresy. Many heretics of the previous centuries had also been accused of being witches. In addition, a growing number of religious thinkers and writers—including Thomas Aquinas, a leading thirteenth-century scholar—were taking magic and sorcery seriously. They argued that heresy and sorcery came from the same source: the devil. Magic *did* exist, and it was evil. Witches' powers could only have been acquired through pacts, or agreements, with the devil or the evil spirits who served him. In 1374 Pope Gregory XI made this view official when he declared that all magic required the help of demons. Anyone who practiced magic, therefore, was guilty of heresy. The professors of the University of Paris added their opinion in 1398, announcing that magic was real . . . and dangerous.

Witchcraft was no longer simply pagan superstition, outside the realm of Christian thought. It was anti-Christian, the enemy of the church and of society. The system of inquisitors, torturers, ecclesiastical courts, and executioners that had been created to punish heretics could also be used against witches. In 1484 Pope Innocent VIII gave the inquisitors permission to go after witches. The stage was set for the witch hunts.

The New Science of Demonology

Many witch trials took place in Europe before 1484. In Ireland in 1324, for example, a bishop accused Lady Alice Kyteler, her son, and her maid of witchcraft. The evidence came from the maid, who was whipped a half dozen times before she confessed. Although Lady Alice and her son paid fines and survived, the maid was burned. But such trials were scattered, isolated events, and the number of people accused was small. During the fifteenth century, the witch hunts grew into much larger affairs. Spreading

Witches dance at a gathering and burn sacrificial victims in this sixteenth-century Swiss illustration.

waves of accusations plunged whole communities into mass trials that led to mass executions. Fueling the fire of these witch panics was a string of books on demonology.

Demon comes from the Greek word *daimon,* which referred to any supernatural being less than a god, whether it was good, evil, or neutral. In Christian usage, though, all demons were evil. The study of demons' actions—especially of their dealings with witches—came to be called demonology. Books on the subject, which often contained material from witches' confessions, served as manuals for the inquisitors. The books told how witches behaved, what signs to look for in cases of sorcery, and how to torture and punish witches.

Although demonological texts started appearing in the late fourteenth century, a book published in 1487 was probably more influential than any other, shaping people's ideas about witchcraft and urging them to take action against witches. That book was the *Malleus Maleficarum* (*Hammer of Witches,* or, literally, *Hammer of Evildoers*), usually credited to the German monks and inquisitors Heinrich Krämer and Jacob Sprenger, although many modern researchers question whether Sprenger actually contributed to the work. One of the most significant features of the *Malleus Maleficarum* was its attack on women. It did not claim that all witches were women, but it did say that women were weaker than men, more likely to sin, and more easily manipulated by the devil.

New demonological books kept appearing throughout the sixteenth century and beyond. They reinforced the ideas that witches existed, that they worshipped the devil at secret meetings called sabbats, and that they posed a grave threat to public safety. Many of these books were written by judges who had overseen witch trials. For example, Nicholas Rémy, a French judge who published a book called *Demonolatria* (Demon Worship) in 1595, boasted of having killed nine hundred witches. Pierre de Lancre, the chief inquisitor of the French province of Bordeaux, complained in his 1612 text on demonology that he had been able to kill only six hundred. James VI, king of Scotland, wrote a demonological book and encouraged witch trials in Scotland. When he later became King James I of England, he toughened the English

> MALLEVS
> MALEFICARVM,
> MALEFICAS ET EARVM
> hæresim framceâ conterens,
> EX VARIIS AVCTORIBVS COMPILATVS,
> & in quatuor Tomos iustè distributus,
> QVORVM DVO PRIORES VANAS DÆMONVM
> versutias, præstigiosas eorum delusiones, superstitiosas Strigimagarum
> cæremonias, horrendos etiam cum illis congressus; exactam denique
> tam pestiferæ sectæ disquisitionem, & punitionem complectuntur.
> Tertius praxim Exorcistarum ad Dæmonum, & Strigimagarum male-
> ficia de Christi fidelibus pellenda; Quartus verò Artem Doctrinalem,
> Benedictionalem, & Exorcismalem continent.
> TOMVS PRIMVS.
> Indices Auctorum, capitum, rerúmque non desunt.
> Editio nouissima, infinitis penè mendis expurgata; cuique accessit Fuga
> Dæmonum & Complementum artis exorcisticæ.
> Vir sine mulier, in quibus Pythonicus, vel diuinationis fuerit spiritus, morte moriatur
> Leuitici cap. 10.
>
> LVGDVNI,
> Sumptibus CLAVDII BOVRGEAT, sub signo Mercurij Galli.
> M. DC. LXIX.
> CVM PRIVILEGIO REGIS.

The *Hammer of Witches* was first published in Germany in 1487, about forty years after the printing press was invented. The new technology let this guide for witch-hunters spread rapidly.

laws against witchcraft. This led to an increase in witch hunts and trials.

Not all learned people of the time accepted demonology. In the early sixteenth century the German scholar Heinrich Cornelius von Nettenheim, called Agrippa, criticized the inquistors' methods and defended women who were accused of being witches. French writer Cyrano de Bergerac wrote a public letter in 1654, mocking belief in witchcraft as superstition.

Speaking up against demonology and witch hunts could be dangerous. Englishman Reginald Scot published *The Discoverie of Witchcraft* (1584), which argued that witchcraft was a delusion and that witch trials were un-Christian. King James had Scot's book burned. A few years later, a Dutch scholar named Cornelius Loos said that demons weren't real and that the witch hunts were a mistake. Peter Binsfield, a bishop and witch-hunter, threw Loos into prison. Only after Loos said on his knees that he was wrong was he released. Later, though, Loos was imprisoned in another city, where he died in jail.

Despite the risk of drawing the inquisitors' wrath, skeptical or humane individuals continued to criticize the witch mania. Alonzo de Salazar Frias of Spain started out as an investigator of witchcraft in northern Spain, a mountainous region inhabited by the Basque people, who had a reputation as sorcerers. Salazar Frias found no evidence of real witchcraft and became a skeptic. In the early seventeenth century he urged Spanish civil and religious authorities to halt the persecution of witches in Spain, and although Pierre de Lancre and other witch-hunters protested, the Spanish Inquisition soon stopped trying people as witches.

Near the end of the seventeenth century, Dutch scholar Balthasar Bekker published *De Betoverde Weereld* (The Enchanted World, 1691), which denied the reality of demons and criticized belief in witchcraft. Bekker lost his position in the church, but many people read his book, which helped bring the era of the witch hunts to a close.

Witch Hunts: Myths and Truths

Misinformation and misunderstanding surround the European witch hunts. Since the 1970s, however, new research has cast light on this dark chapter in history. Some of the most useful studies have focused on old trial records preserved in city and national archives. Through the difficult, painstaking work of reviewing thousands of pages of dusty documents, researchers are piecing together a more accurate picture.

Historians now know that there was nothing "medieval" about the witch hunts. Large-scale witch panics began in the fourteenth century, at the end of the Middle Ages. They reached their height during the Renaissance and continued into the eighteenth century, an era sometimes called the Enlightenment or the Age of Reason. Witchcraft persecution was most intense between about 1560 and 1630.

Although the idea of witches as heretics and devil worshippers originated in Roman Catholic thought, witch hunts cannot be blamed entirely on the Roman Catholic Church. After the Protestant sects of Christianity split away from Catholicism in the middle of the witch-hunt era, Protestants tried and executed witches just as eagerly Catholics did. And the campaign against witchcraft wasn't carried out by the churches alone. Inquisitors and ecclesiastical courts depended on the cooperation of civil governments, soldiers and jailers, and ordinary citizens. Belief in witches—and the desire to exterminate them—was shared by all classes of society, including many of the most highly educated people of the time.

A suspected witch is weighed on a scale. Witches were believed to be unnaturally light because they lacked souls.

Nearly all European countries saw at least one large witch hunt. Germany had the greatest number of mass trials and executions. Mass trials were also numerous in eastern France, western Switzerland, northern Italy, and Scotland. In contrast, England, the Netherlands, Scandinavia, Spain, Portugal, and southern Italy had fewer mass trials and executions, although individual trials and punishments were common in some places.

How many people died in the witch hunts? One figure that crops up again and again is 9 million. It first appeared in the 1893 book *Woman, Church, and State,* written by an American feminist named Matilda Joslyn Gage, and was later repeated by many other sources. Unfortunately, Gage's figure was sheer guesswork, and it is dramatically wrong. One of the most important achievements of recent witch-hunt scholarship is an accurate estimate of the death toll. Historians now think that between 100,000 and 110,000 people stood trial between the fourteenth and eighteenth centuries. Of these, 40,000 to 60,000 were executed.

Methods of execution varied. Some witches were burned alive at stakes, but many more were hanged (although sometimes their corpses were burned afterward). Witches were also beheaded and drowned. Some died under torture, but torture was almost never used as a method of execution. People who were convicted of witchcraft might be punished rather than executed. Depending upon the local laws, punishments included imprisonment, fines, banishment from the community or from the country, whipping, and branding.

The image of the witch as an old woman, probably poor and unpopular, possibly a "white witch" or healer, is something of a misconception, if not quite a myth. Between 20 and 25 percent of all accused witches were men. In some places, such as Scandinavia and Iceland, half or more were men. Although many accused witches were poor folk who lived on the outskirts of society and were widely disliked, others belonged to the middle and even upper classes. Some healers and wisewomen were charged with witchcraft, but in other cases such women made the accusations against others, or worked with the witch-hunters.

Modern historians have learned that there was no such thing as a "typical" witch, and no single group seems to have been targeted for persecution. Still, many historians agree that an older woman, especially a woman without a husband and children, or one who depended upon charity for her support, was at higher than normal risk of being accused.

A witch hunt or trial started with rumors or accusations of *maleficium*—wrongdoing through sorcery. Usually this meant that someone complained that something bad had happened. The most common complaints involved sickness, the death of children or livestock, crops that failed, bad weather, lost property, disputes over the inheritance of property, and other matters of daily life.

Once suspicions of witchcraft were in the air, the matter could be taken up by the local clergy, judges, or inquisitors. The person who originally made the complaint might be concerned primarily with his sick cow or her missing silver spoon, but the authorities were much more interested in the diabolical or satanic aspects of witchcraft: the night flights, the sabbats, the cannibalism, and all the other horrid acts that the demonologists described. Their chief interest was in proving that a witch had sworn allegiance to the devil.

Seated in the ducking stool, repeatedly held underwater, some suspects were tortured into confessing witchcraft.

A person being investigated for witchcraft might undergo certain tests. One old-fashioned test was called the ordeal by water. Seldom used after the fifteenth century, it involved throwing a witch into a river or pond. This test could be interpreted in different ways. According to one system, anyone who drowned was guilty. Someone who didn't drown might still be guilty, but guilt wasn't proven. In a different version of the ordeal, anyone who sank was innocent (and might be able to be rescued from the water). Someone who didn't sink was guilty, because the water wouldn't accept one of the devil's servants.

Another test involved the "witch's mark." Demonologists said that every witch bore the mark of the devil somewhere on his or her body. The mark could be a bump, a mole, or a patch of discolored skin. Because no one has perfect skin all over, inquisitors were generally able to find a witch's mark on a suspect. A witch was supposed to be unable to feel pain at the site of the mark, so the suspect's eyes would be covered, and the inquisitors would touch the mark several times with a blunt pin and then with a sharp one. If the suspect cried out in pain at the sharp pinprick, he or she was not a witch. There were, however, ways to ensure that the suspect didn't feel the pin. One of the most notorious witch-hunters, Matthew Hopkins of seventeenth-century England, was discov-

ered using a trick pin with a retractable point. The suspects he tested with this false device had no way of knowing when to cry out. Each time, Hopkins could announce that he had "found" another witch.

If the examiners determined that someone was likely to be a witch, the next step was obtaining a confession that would seal the conviction. Normal rules that limited the use of torture were stretched—or suspended altogether—in the case of witchcraft. The methods used against witches were so horrible that many

For Matthew Hopkins, "witch finding" was a business. Towns paid him a bounty for each witch he discovered.

accused people confessed immediately rather than undergo torture, called the "hard question." But even after confessing, a witch might be tortured, just to confirm the confession. As Johannes Junius of Bamberg discovered, inquisitors particularly wanted to hear the names of other witches.

Today it is common to think of the victims of the witch hunts as tragic, innocent figures. Some small percentage of those who confessed to witchcraft probably did practice sorcery and may have believed that they really were witches. Perhaps, in their own minds, they really were guilty. Yet never was there any evidence that witchcraft had actually caused harm. Nor was there a shred of evidence of the thing demonologists and authorities feared most: a vast conspiracy of witches working on behalf of the devil to overthrow Christianity and civilization.

What caused the witch hunts? For more than a century people have pondered that question. Dozens of possibilities have been suggested, from social stress caused by religious conflict to mass delusions caused by spoiled food. In the end, no single explanation applies to all cases. From the point of view of the twenty-first century, only one thing about the witch hunts is clear: the fear was real.

Inside a Witch Trial: The Fatal Feud

One of the most talked-about witch trials in England was the case of the Pendle witches. It took place in 1612, after years of accusations and counteraccusations between feuding families. The Pendle witch trial was the largest mass trial held in England up to that time. Filled with drama and terrifying claims, it received wide publicity and influenced other trials in the years that followed.

The scene was the Pendle Forest, in the eastern part of the Lancashire district. At the time, Lancashire was an uneasy place. The local population was mostly Roman Catholic, but England was officially Protestant. A history of Catholic plots against the government had led authorities to regard all Catholics as potential traitors. As a result there was tension between Catholics and Protestants, which made itself felt in every aspect of community life.

Pendle Forest was home to two peasant clans, each headed by an old woman believed to be a witch. One of these women was Elizabeth Sowthern, a blind beggar whom everyone called Old Demdike. The other was a "withered, spent, and decrepit creature" named Anne Whittle, generally known as Old Chattox. Unkempt

Witches crept into hundreds of legends and folktales. Dulle Griet, a witch in a Dutch story, stole the treasure of hell, unafraid of its monsters.

and quarrelsome, the two women matched the popular image of the witch as an ancient hag. They were rumored to lead a coven of witches in the forest, and they seem to have encouraged the community to believe that they were witches so that they could do business in herbal potions and medicines.

The two women were friends until, around 1601, some grain and clothing were stolen from Alison Device, Sowthern's granddaughter. Device then claimed that she saw the missing clothing being worn by Whittle's daughter, Anne Redfearne. The two older women argued bitterly, starting a feud between their families. At some point Alison Device's father, John Device, agreed to pay Whittle a certain amount of grain every year. This agreement patched things up for a while, until John Device died.

By early 1612 the feud was again going strong. The business came to the attention of Roger Nowell, a justice of the peace. Nowell investigated the matter and received a mass of complaints, each side accusing the other of all manner of wicked witchcraft. Nowell imprisoned Sowthern, Whittle, and Redfearne in Lancaster Castle to await trial. Soon Alison Device was also imprisoned for cursing a traveling salesman who had refused to give her some pins. He had collapsed—probably from a stroke, although Device said that she had caused his collapse and permanent disability.

Before the trial began, the suspects hurled volleys of accusations at each other in the hope of shifting the blame. Their declarations (and sometimes confessions) were sensational. Elizabeth Sowthern admitted that she had been a witch for many years, ever since meeting "a spirit or devil in the shape of a boy" and giving him her soul in exchange for anything she wanted. (No one seems to have asked why, if this were true, she hadn't taken advantage of the diabolical bargain to escape life as a blind old beggar.) After she made this pact, the devil sometimes appeared to her in the form of a brown dog or a black cat. Later Sowthern had taught her children and grandchildren to be witches. Whittle had also become a witch by selling her soul, as had several family members and neighbors.

Eventually eleven people stood trial. Sowthern and Whittle were charged with using sorcery to commit murder, although Sowthern died in prison before the trial began. Another set of charges was leveled at various family members who were accused of plotting to blow up Lancaster Castle in order to rescue the prisoners. These and other members of the supposed coven were charged with using sorcery to inflict pain, drive people mad, and do murder. The deaths thought to be from sorcery totalled sixteen.

The case against the Pendle witches was based on the testimony of several members of Sowthern's family. One of them was a nine-year-old girl

A man tries to capture a witch in this English drawing from around 1600. Witches were often said to live in forests, like the old women of Pendle.

named Jannet Device, Sowthern's granddaughter. She should not have been allowed to testify at all, because English law banned the use of statements from children under the age of fourteen. The court used her testimony anyway, and it was colorful. Jannet said that her mother's familiar was a brown dog named Ball. She also said that her mother had killed at least three people using a very common form of witchcraft called image magic. Sowthern had left an account of how this could be done, in words that echo the ancient Mesopotamian "burning" ritual of the figurines:

> *The speediest way to take a man's life away by witchcraft is to make a picture of clay, like unto the shape of the person whom they mean to kill, and dry it thoroughly. And when you would have them to be ill in any one place more than another, then take a thorn or pin and prick it in that part of the picture you would so have to be ill. And when you would have any part of the body to consume away, then take that part of the picture and burn it. And so thereupon by that means the body shall die.*

At the end of the Pendle case, ten people were hanged as witches in Lancaster on August 20, 1612. Another member of the coven had already been hanged in another town, and a twelfth member, whose only crime was causing the death of a horse through witchcraft, was spared execution, although she went to jail. The next year Thomas Potts, clerk of the court that had tried the Pendle witches, published a book about the case. Certified accurate by the judge in charge, the book was called *The Wonderful Discovery of Witches in the County of Lancaster.* It spread the details of the Pendle witch accusations across northern England, to be repeated by accusers in later witch panics.

One of those panics broke out right in Pendle Forest. In 1634 a young boy charged several women with witchcraft. Jannet Device, who had testified against her family when she was nine, was one of the accused. But after the boy admitted that he had made up the story of witchcraft, the women—unlike Old Demdike, Old Chattox, and the others twenty-two years earlier—were set free.

Condemned as a witch, a Salem woman being led to her execution looks innocent and tragic in this painting from the nineteenth century. By that time, fear of witches had given way to questions about how the witch trials could have happened.

Panic in America

Toward the end of the seventeenth century, the witch panics were dying down in England, Germany, France, and other European nations. But the fear had not yet disappeared, and in 1692 it flared up with terrible results across the Atlantic. This American witch hunt took place in the Massachusetts Bay Colony. Its heart was a place called Salem Village.

"Under an Evil Hand"

It started with two girls who lived in the house of the Reverend Samuel Parris, minister of Salem Village. One was his nine-year-old daughter Betty. The other was his niece Abigail, who was three or four years older than Betty. In January the girls complained of feeling ill and started acting very strangely. They stared into empty corners of rooms, cried out at nothing, babbled sentences that didn't mean anything, and twisted their bodies into unnatural positions. In the words of the seventeenth century, they were "having fits."

Parris's prayers didn't cure the girls of their fits. The local doctor, William Griggs, couldn't cure them either, but he did decide what was wrong with them. He announced that Betty and Abigail

Cotton Mather, one of the best-known ministers in the American colonies, believed that witchcraft was real.

were "under an evil hand." Everyone knew exactly what he meant.

Three years earlier, a leading New England minister named Cotton Mather had published a extremely popular book called *Memorable Providences.* This book described the case of the Goodwin children of Boston, who had suffered fits just like those of Betty and Abigail. The Goodwin children had accused a servant woman of bewitching them. After the servant was hanged as a witch, the children's fits ended. People in Salem Village were sure that the same thing had happened to Betty and Abigail— they were under a witch's spell. And they weren't the only ones. Four of their friends were now having witch-caused fits, too. But who was the witch behind the fits?

Before long the girls were naming names. They accused three women: Tituba, a black West Indian who was one of the Reverend Parris's slaves; Sarah Good, a homeless beggar; and Sarah Osburn, an older woman who had caused gossip in the community when she upset the social order by marrying her servant. The local magistrates, or judges, examined all three women in the Salem Village meetinghouse.

Tituba said that Parris had beaten her and ordered her to confess. And confess she did, in great detail. She said that she had had dealings with the devil and that Good and Osburn were witches, too. All three women went to jail, but the magistrates were convinced that an unholy conspiracy remained to be uprooted. They wanted to find the other witches of the coven.

The girls next accused Martha Corey, a respected member of the community and the church. She was examined, then imprisoned. Ann Putnam was one of the four girls who had joined Betty and Abigail in having fits, and now her mother, also named Ann Putnam, appeared to be a victim, too.

More accusations followed. Among those named were Rebecca Nurse, age seventy-one; Sarah Good's four-year-old daughter; and several married couples. By the end of April, nearly thirty people were in jail. The following month the colony's new governor, Sir William Phips, arrived from England. He appointed a court to hear the witchcraft cases. William Stoughton, the deputy governor, was the chief judge.

The trials began on June 2. Eight days later, the first of the convicted witches, Bridget Bishop, was hanged. One of the judges resigned in protest over the use of "spectral evidence"—that is, statements by the victims of witchcraft that they could see things that were invisible to others. During the trials, for example, the girls who made the accusations often shrieked and pointed at the ceiling or at some other empty spot, claiming to see such things as a yellow bird, a familiar spirit to some of the witches. The girls also writhed and twisted in their seats, crying out that "specters" in the images of the accused witches were pinching, choking, or slapping them. The idea behind spectral evidence was that the devil could not use a person's likeness to form a specter unless that person were a witch. Stoughton supported the use of such "evidence," even though it had never before been used to decide guilt or innocence.

Concerned that the trials should be properly conducted, Phips consulted with the leading ministers of Boston, including Cotton Mather and his father, Increase Mather. The Mathers sent back a document called "The Return of the Ministers Consulted," which

The Salem trials were full of fainting, shrieking, and spirit sightings by those who claimed to be tormented by witches.

told the investigators to proceed with caution but also to take "speedy and vigorous" action against accused witches. The investigators were also advised not to rely on spectral evidence alone. Yet apart from confessions, spectral evidence was the *only* evidence.

By this time, the girls' accusations had spread beyond Salem Village. People in nearby communities had asked them to come and reveal any witches there. As a result, accused witches in Salem Town were in jail awaiting trial. So were residents of Andover, Ipswich, Cambridge, and Boston. Some of the accused were leading citizens of the colony, including John Alden, a well-known sea captain, and Philip English, the richest merchant in Salem.

Five more convicted witches, all women, were hanged in mid-July, and many more were brought to trial. The accused were under great pressure—including torture in some cases—to confess that they had made bargains with the devil. The court's use of the confessions, however, differed from the normal practice in witch trials such as that of Johannes Junius of Bamberg. People who confessed were spared immediate execution, while those who refused to confess were sentenced to die.

Why, then, didn't everyone confess? No doubt many of the accused were genuinely horrified by the idea of saying they had had dealings with the devil. In addition, they did not know that such a confession wouldn't be used against them in the future. More than 160 people were accused, but only 47 confessed.

Four men and a woman were hanged in mid-August. On September 17, nine people were sentenced to death. A man named Giles Corey, who refused to plead either innocent or guilty and therefore could not stand trial, was put to torture. He was forced to lie down with a board on top of his body. Stones were placed on the board, slowly increasing the weight. After two days of this, Corey died. Three days later,

Accusations of witchcraft tore apart communities, turning neighbor against neighbor.

The Wonders of the Invisible World:

Being an Account of the

T R Y A L S

OF

Several Witches,

Lately Excuted in

N E W - E N G L A N D :

And of several remarkable Curiosities therein Occurring.

Together with,

I. Observations upon the Nature, the Number, and the Operations of the Devils.

II. A short Narrative of a late outrage committed by a knot of Witches in *Swede-Land*, very much resembling, and so far explaining, that under which *New-England* has laboured.

III. Some Councels directing a due Improvement of the Terrible things lately done by the unusual and amazing Range of *Evil-Spirits* in *New-England*.

IV. A brief Discourse upon those *Temptations* which are the more ordinary Devices of Satan.

By *COTTON MATHER.*

Published by the Special Command of his EXCELLENCY the Govenour of the Province of the *Massachusetts-Bay* in *New-England.*

Printed first, at *Bostun* in *New-England;* and Reprinted at *London,* for *John Dunton,* at the *Raven* in the *Poultry.* 1693.

The year after the Salem trials, Cotton Mather published this account of them.

six women and two men were hanged, bringing the total of hangings to nineteen. At least five others died in jail due to mistreatment and harsh conditions.

At this point, many people in the colony were having second thoughts about the witch trials. When the girls started accusing such highly placed individuals as the governor's wife, the tide turned. Increase Mather delivered a sermon against spectral evidence, saying, "It were better that ten suspected witches should escape, than that one innocent person should be condemned." A few days later, a respected Boston merchant and scientist named Thomas Brattle wrote a letter for public circulation. It strongly criticized the trials, especially the girls' visions of specters. The public was clearly turning against the trials.

In mid-October Governor Phips ordered a halt to the executions and imprisonments. Soon afterward he disbanded the special witchcraft court. In early 1693 all remaining suspects were released. The nightmare was over.

In the aftermath of the trials, many people blamed Samuel Parris for letting the whole business get started. He had leaped on the idea that Betty and Abigail were bewitched and had worked hard to convince others it was true. Although Parris did admit that he might have been mistaken, he insisted that he had done nothing wrong. He managed to hold on to his position as minister of Salem Village, but only until 1696, when he was forced to leave.

The years that followed saw a slow trickle of apologies, as magistrates and jurors who had convicted their neighbors of witchcraft tried to explain what had happened. One of the most significant public statements came in 1706 when Ann Putnam, one of the girls who had been most active in making accusations, stood in church while the minister read her apology aloud. Putnam said that it had all been "a great delusion of Satan."

"These Mysterious Troubles"

By 1692, when the Salem witch panic broke out, the backlash against witch-hunting was under way in Europe. People were taking a more critical look at the notion of demonic magic and diabolical pacts. In England, the colony's parent country, the witch craze had largely faded away. So what happened in Salem?

As with the European witch hunts in general, historians have filled whole bookshelves with theories about the events in Salem. And as with the witch hunts in general, no single explanation is accepted by everyone.

The Salem witchcraft case raises two related but separate questions: What caused the girls to make their accusations in the first place? And why were the accusations so readily accepted by so many people in the colony?

The second question may be easier to think about than the first. In the late seventeenth century the Massachusetts Bay Colony was filled with social, economic, and political tension. Divisions were forming between rural villagers and farmers on one hand, and the urban elite of growing Boston on the other. Differences between wealth and poverty led to resentment and spite. The colony's political status—its very survival—seemed uncertain. Until Phips arrived from England, Massachusetts was without a governor and

The devil instructs young witches in this illustration from the *Compendium Maleficarum*, an influential 1626 work on demonology.

a royal charter to guarantee its continuation. Leadership was in question, and people were fearful about the future. Insecurity, envy, and rivalry could have made them turn on one another.

Religion played a key part, too. There is no doubt that people believed in the existence of the devil and his desire to attack Christians. As for witchcraft, their own religious leaders had assured them that witches did exist, and people had already been hanged for witchcraft in Massachusetts. It was the size of the Salem case, not the fact that it happened, that made it stand out in North American history.

Religion not only provided a basis for belief in witchcraft but also produced stress in the colony. The Puritans who had settled Massachusetts clung so strictly to their beliefs that any difference of opinion or custom created a disturbance. Salem Village, in particular, had been troubled by disagreements among the faithful.

In the sixteen years before the trials, three ministers had had to leave the village because of disputes. When Parris arrived, he was not welcomed by all—in fact, the committee of village leaders disapproved of Parris and withheld his payment for months. The village was divided between those who liked and supported Parris and those who were opposed to him. The accusers all came from families friendly to Parris, but none of the supposed witches did.

It is possible that village politics played into the witchcraft panic, which simply got out of hand. Psychology, the science of the mind, has shown that once rumors and accusations are in the air, they are contagious. People are often afraid to speak out against the majority view—especially when they risk their own imprisonment and execution by doing so.

But what about the girls themselves? Why did they make their wild accusations?

Mental illness, food poisoning, and religious hysteria have been put forward as possible explanations for their behavior. But there is a simpler possibility. Maybe the children simply started out with a lie, perhaps meant as nothing more than a prank, and then kept it up, either because they enjoyed the attention or because they were afraid to stop. We will never know for sure what was in their minds, but Thomas Brattle's letter about the trials tells us quite clearly what he thought:

These afflicted persons [the girls] do say, and have often declared it, that they can see spectres when their eyes are shut, as well as when they are open. This is one thing I evermore accounted as very observable, and that which might serve as a good key to unlock the nature of these mysterious troubles, if duly improved by us. Can they see spectres when their eyes are shut? I am sure they lie, at least speak falsely, if they say so; for the thing, in nature, is an utter impossibility. It is true, they may strongly fancy, or have things represented to their imagination, when their eyes are shut; and I think this is all which ought to be allowed to these blind, nonsensical girls; and if our officers and courts have apprehended, imprisoned, condemned, and executed our guiltless neighbours, certainly our error is great, and we shall rue [regret] it in conclusion.

Some people today embrace Wicca, a religion based on
traditional witchcraft practices and beliefs.

Witches of the New Age

"The sun is low and golden, near to sinking. The women who are to dance the reaping emerge in black robes, crowns of ripened wheat and poppies on their heads. Each holds a silver sickle whose blade turns to gold in the evening light." Vivianne Crowley, a priestess of Wicca, is describing a ceremony held on one of the eight seasonal festivals that many modern witches celebrate.

This particular ceremony took place in 1995, at sunset on July 31, which is the beginning of the Wiccan festival called Lughnasadh or Lammas. This festival marks the point in the cycle of seasons when wheat is harvested. It is summer, but fall is on the way, and the days are growing shorter—a reminder that, as Crowley says, people as well as wheat "grow, mature, peak, and then decline." Lughnasadh, she explains, "can be a healing time, a time to let go of the negative energy of illness." Perhaps the connection with sickness was especially mean- ingful to Crowley that year because one of the people celebrating Lugh- nasadh with her was a friend named Stephen, who was seriously ill.

Before the ceremony started, the men in the group had drawn straws to see which one of them would take the role of the Lammas god, who represents the wheat that is sacrificed to make food. Stephen drew the shortest straw. He would represent the Lammas god.

Then the women came forth in their black robes, bearing the silver sickles. (A sickle is a curved blade, an old-fashioned tool for reaping wheat, or cutting it by hand.) They formed a circle, saluted the four directions of the compass, and began to dance. As they danced, they waved their sickles as though reaping. When the dance ended, the women surrounded the men and clashed their sickle blades together. Stephen fell to the ground. The others covered him with a black cloth to symbolize death, then scattered wheat and poppies over it. As the sun set they chanted:

He shall be cut down in the wheat for me,
sustenance shall he be to all.
Take these, the gifts of our hand and heart,
and bear our secret wishes to the gods.
Dark Mother, Earth Mother, take him to your embrace.

A second chant summoned the dead god to be reborn. He would rise again as new wheat grows in place of the old:

Die not but live,
fall not, but renew.

The black cloth fell away. Stephen stood up. The ritual of sacrifice, offering, and rebirth was complete. Soon afterward, Crowley says, Stephen's doctors introduced a new form of medical treatment, and he got better.

Changing Images

The ceremonies of Wiccans like Crowley and her friends are part of a modern revival of magical thinking in Great Britain, the

United States, and other industrialized countries. The image of the witch, which has taken so many forms, is still evolving today, and Wicca is one of its new faces.

As the waves of panic and hysteria that had caused the witch hunts died away, the idea of demonic witchcraft lost its hold on courts and communities. Starting in the eighteenth century, reason and science led people away from belief in witchcraft. The witch, no longer respected or feared, faded from the scene. But although people had lost their fear of witches in real life, they seemed to be more fascinated than ever with witches in fiction. From

Even though belief faded, witches held their place in stories like "Hansel and Gretel."

the cannibal witch of the Brothers Grimm's "Hansel and Gretel" to the Wicked Witch of the West in *The Wizard of Oz* and the Witch of the Waste in *Howl's Moving Castle,* witches have added menace, mystery, and even humor to popular entertainment.

A new view of historical witchcraft also emerged in the first half of the twentieth century. A 1921 book called *The Witch-Cult in Western Europe,* by an Egyptologist named Margaret Murray, put forward the theory that European witchcraft was the remnant of an ancient pagan religion that had been replaced by Christianity. Murray was right, in a way—witchcraft belief does include many elements that echo a variety of ancient religions and folklores. But Murray was incorrect in her claim that a single, widespread, fertility-worshipping religion dating from the Stone Age survived through the Middle Ages, unrecorded

Gerald Gardner is considered the father of modern Wicca, although his scholarship was shaky.

by any ancient or medieval writers, and was finally exposed and almost wiped out by the witch hunts.

Modern researchers have strongly criticized Murray's careless use of unreliable and inadequate source material. She based her ideas more on imagination than on proof. No evidence from archaeology or old documents shows an unbroken connection between ancient religion and fifteenth-century witch covens. Yet in spite of the flaws in Murray's work, her idea entered the public mind and influenced other writers. One of them was Gerald B. Gardner, a retired British government employee who, in the 1940s, created the modern form of witchcraft called Wicca.

Gardner claimed to belong to a witch coven that traced its ancestry to the era of the witch hunts. Through his Museum of Magic and Witchcraft and books such as *Witchcraft Today* (1954), Gardner shared a detailed vision of ideas and practices that he called traditional witchcraft. Most of what Gardner said about witchcraft can be found in earlier works on folklore and magic. His attempt to show an unbroken connection between pre-Christian beliefs and modern witches is no more convincing than Murray's, and it is unclear whether he actually knew any people who claimed to practice the "ancient religion." Gardner did, however, create an imaginative basis for the rebirth of witchcraft known as Wicca.

Another important influence on Wicca (and on Neopaganism, or new paganism, which has many elements in common with Wicca) was *The White Goddess*, a 1948 book by the British poet Robert

Graves. Treading the line between fact and fiction, *The White Goddess* explored the idea that an ancient goddess-worshipping cult could lie hidden, almost lost and forgotten, behind European culture and religion. Together with the work of Murray, Gardner, and other mid-twentieth-century writers who speculated about magic and mythology, Graves's book promoted the vision of a pre-Christian goddess religion that practiced magic. *The White Goddess* has inspired numerous modern works of fiction, such as Marion Zimmer Bradley's *The Mists of Avalon* (1982). It also helped shape Wicca.

The Life of a Modern Witch

In the past half century or so, Wicca has evolved into many versions. Most of its practitioners define it as an Earth-centered, nature-worshipping, magical religion. Depending on the form of Wicca they follow, Wiccans may worship a goddess, a god, both, or multiple deities. And although Wiccans and Neopagans are careful to explain that they are not devil worshippers, some other modern groups do recognize Satan as their deity, or one of their deities.

No one knows how many Wiccans and Neopagans there are in the United States or the world. In their 1999 book *Witchcraft: Exploring the World of Wicca*, Helen Berger and Craig Hawkins estimated the number of Wiccans in America at 150,000 to 200,000. Other sources have arrived at similar figures. But that same year, a Wiccan Web site called *The Witch's Voice* claimed that there were a million Wiccans, witches, and Neopagans in the United States and 3 million worldwide. In 2006 a Wiccan in Portland, Oregon, suggested that all estimates are likely to be faulty. "We witches are like cats," he said. "Many of us are solitary, and even when we do get together in groups, we don't stand still long enough to be counted."

Wiccans and other modern witches often approach their prac-

At a Wicca school in Illinois, Wiccans take part in a lunar ritual. Modern witches regard the moon as a symbol of wisdom and power.

tices in individualistic, creative ways. Most of them, though, share certain basic beliefs and customs, whether they practice on their own or in groups, churches, or covens. In *Confessions of a Teenage Witch* (2005), Gwinevere Rain describes some of the key elements of the Craft, as many modern witches call witchcraft.

One element is the Craft name, a name chosen when someone adopts the Wiccan way. Another is the Book of Shadows, a personal journal for notes, reflections, and spells. Many Wiccans also use tools for divination, which is the art of foretelling the future or finding the answers to questions. Tarot cards and crystal balls, for example, are divination tools, although many Wiccans use simpler methods, such as gazing into a bowl of water.

Circle casting is central to Wiccan practices. A Wiccan who intends to perform a ritual or spell does so inside a circle that has been marked with cord, stones, or chalk, or perhaps simply visualized. Items representing the four ancient elements are placed in the circle at the four compass points: north for earth, east for air, south for fire, and west for water. At gatherings for Wiccan festivals such as the Lughnasadh celebration, the circle may be large enough to contain many people.

Hundreds of books and Web sites offer detailed—and sometimes conflicting—information about magical and Wiccan practices. The popularity of the subject in the early years of the twenty-first century suggests that witchcraft may be on the rise, as many Wiccans claim. To some people, though, witchcraft remains as mysterious, even scary, as it has been for thousands of years.

Gwinevere Rain, for example, tells of an incident that took place at school when she was fifteen years old, after she had "come out of the broom closet" to her friends as a Wiccan. When a girl in her social studies class got upset with an obnoxious boy, she pointed at Rain and said to the boy, "Watch out or she'll put a curse on you." Rain wrote later, "I don't mind that everyone knows about me being Wiccan. I just don't want people to believe in the stereotype of practitioners cursing other people."

Minister Selena Fox performs a ceremony during a Wiccan rally in 2006.

Yet Wicca is just one of the more recent chapters in the long history of the witch. The word *witch* conjures up a host of images: the flesh-nibbling hags of Thessaly, the devil-worshipping night fliers so desperately feared during the age of the witch hunts, the village wisewomen with their healing herbs, the cackling crones of fairy tales, and the nature-loving priests and priestesses of a new religion. Belief in witchcraft is clearly not dead. Who knows what the witch might yet become?

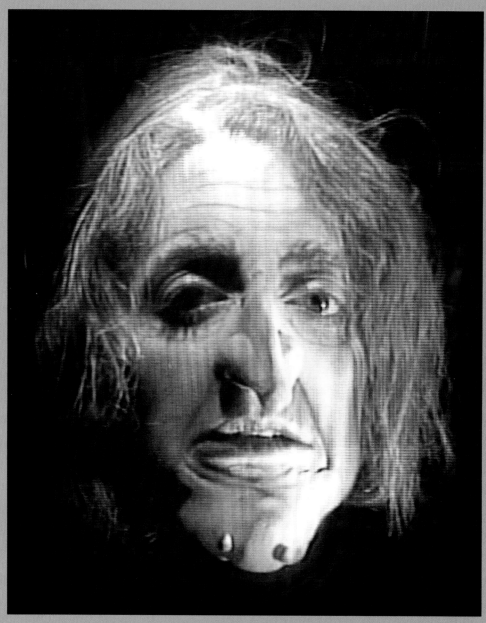

Hideous and menacing, this traditional image of a witch
haunts the imagination and appears in many stories and movies,
yet it is as artificial as a Halloween mask. Throughout
history, witches have fit no single pattern.

What Do You Think?

Salem, Massachusetts, now calls itself the Witch Capital of the World. Relics of the witchcraft trials, including a monument to the dead and a museum of witchcraft, are tourist attractions that draw visitors from around the world.

Many Wiccans and Neopagans make their homes in the Salem area. Each year at the approach of Halloween, the festival known to Wiccans as Samhain, hundreds or thousands more flock to the city to honor the dead witches as victims of fear, superstition, and intolerance. They parade through Old Town in black robes or colorful garb, wearing talismans and carrying candles. On Gallows Hill, where the victims of the Salem trials were hanged, they form a circle and perform a ritual for the nineteen dead. William Stoughton, the judge who presided over the Salem trials, would be astounded by the sight. So would the convicted witches who died there.

Witchcraft in America and the Western world has changed much since the days of the witch hunts. While many devout Christians and members of other religions are deeply disturbed by what they regard as the spiritual dangers of Wicca and witchcraft-related practices, society does not regard witches as a deadly threat. Although parents might try to have witchcraft books banned from libraries, no one suggests stringing up today's witches on Gallows Hill. But in other parts of the world, traditional witchcraft beliefs are still a matter of life and death.

In Saudi Arabia in 2000, a Sudanese man was beheaded in the capital city of Riyadh after being convicted of criminal charges of sorcery. He had claimed to be able to heal sick people and "separate married couples." In 2002, the superintendent of police of India's Rangareddi district led an investigation into crimes based on fear of *banamati,* the local term for witchcraft and sorcery. Men and women in various villages in the district had been tortured and mutilated, accused of being witches who had magically made people sick.

Many witchcraft-related crimes in the African nation of Nigeria are committed by the people who call themselves witches, or by those hoping to sell human bodies or organs to witches for use in ritual magic. People have plucked out the eyes from the living, decapitated

Witches in flight, from a French manuscript published in the 15th century, a time when witchcraft seemed all too real.

babies, murdered children and adults, and dismembered corpses, all in the service of sorcery. Often, the practitioners of the crimes believe that their rituals will bring them wealth. In 2006 the southern African nation of Zimbabwe legalized the practice of witchcraft—but only harmless witchcraft. Magic aimed at harming another person remains illegal.

Throughout history, there have probably been more believers in supernatural powers such as witchcraft than there have been skeptics. Despite the lack of any proof that witchcraft has real effects, such beliefs have brought comfort, awe, and empowerment to some people and superstitious terror, pain, and death to others. Do these beliefs have a place in the modern world? Whether you answer that question based on reason, religion, or your own feelings and experiences, you can decide for yourself what, if anything, witchcraft means to you.

Glossary

coven A group of witches that meets to perform rituals together.

demonology The study of demons in order to combat witchcraft, based on the belief that witches are partners of demons or of the devil.

divination Originally, finding the will of the gods; now used more generally to mean fortune-telling, seeing the future, or finding the answers to questions.

magic The supposed power of individuals to control events in the physical and human worlds through secret knowledge or supernatural powers; sometimes spelled *magick* to set it apart from stage magic, which is the performing of illusions for entertainment; may be good and helpful (white magic) or evil and harmful (black magic).

necromancy Communication with the spirits of the dead for purposes of gaining knowledge; sometimes linked to sinful or forbidden knowledge, or practices such as sorcery or black magic.

occult Hidden, secret, mysterious; usually applies to a body of knowledge or to powers.

phenomenon Something unusual or remarkable.

skeptic One who requires extraordinary proof of extraordinary claims and uses critical thinking to test statements.

sorcery Magical practices; often has a negative meaning, as in black magic.

Wicca A belief system that incorporates practices based on white, or good, witchcraft.

witch One who practices witchcraft.

witchcraft The method or art of using magical, supernatural, or mystical powers to influence events and people.

wizard A male witch or magician, although the term *witch* can be used for men as well as women.

For Further Research

Books

Hill, Douglas. *Witches and Magic-Makers.* 2nd ed. New York: Dorling Kindersley, 2000.

Jackson, Shirley. *The Witchcraft of Salem Village.* New York: Random House, 1984.

Kallen, Stuart. *Witches.* San Diego: Lucent, 2000.

Marvel, Laura, ed. *The Salem Witch Trials.* San Diego: Greenhaven, 2003.

McHargue, Georgess. *Meet the Witches.* New York: Lippincott, 1984.

Meltzer, Milton. *Witches and Witch-Hunts: A History of Persecution.* New York: Blue Sky, 1999.

Ogden, Tom. *Wizards and Sorcerers: From Abracadabra to Zoroaster.* New York: Facts on File, 1997.

Rain, Gwinevere. *Confessions of a Teenage Witch: Celebrating the Wiccan Life.* New York: Perigee, 2005.

Roleff, Tamara, ed. *Black Magic and Witches: Fact or Fiction?* San Diego: Greenhaven, 2003.

Ross, Stewart. *Witches.* Brookfield, CT: Copper Beech, 1996.

Saari, Peggy. *Witchcraft in America.* Detroit: UXL, 2001.

Stein, Wendy. *Witches: Opposing Viewpoints.* San Diego: Greenhaven, 1995.

Time-Life Books. *Witches and Witchcraft.* Alexandria, VA: Time-Life Books, 1990.

Web Sites

www.skepdic.com
 * *The Skeptic's Dictionary* is an Internet reference that covers supernatural and paranormal topics "from abracadabra to zombies." Its "Wicca" and "Witch" pages have overviews of the subjects and links to additional sources of information. *The Skeptic's Dictionary* also offers a set of minilessons in critical thinking.

---

*Book or Web site that will help develop critical thinking

etext.virginia.edu/salem/witchcraft/home.html
> *The Salem Witch Trials Documentary Archive*, maintained by the University of Virginia, is an online collection of both primary sources and research material dealing with America's most famous witchcraft cases.

www3.nationalgeographic.com/salem/
> * "Salem Witchcraft Hysteria," created by the National Geographic Society, explores the Salem witch trials in the form of an interactive investigation.

www.cog.org
> The home page of the Covenant of the Goddess, a Wiccan organization, contains information about Wiccan beliefs and activities.

www.religioustolerance.org/witchcra.htm
> From the site of the Ontario Consultants on Religious Tolerance, this page discusses Wicca as a contemporary religion.

www.pbs.org/wnet/secrets/case_salem/clues.html
> * This Web page is based on a PBS *Secrets of the Dead* show that explores ergot poisoning as a possible cause of the witchcraft hysteria in Salem and other places.

historical.library.cornell.edu/witchcraft/index.html
> The Cornell University Library has an online collection of materials about witchcraft, with special focus on the history of superstition and witch hunts in Europe.

departments.kings.edu/womens_history/witch/index.html
> * "The Witch Hunts," part of a women's history site, is a starting point for research into the persecution of witches in Europe between 1400 and 1800. It also offers an interactive witch hunt simulation.

Selected Bibliography

The author found these resources especially helpful when researching and writing this book.

Apps, Lara, and Andrew Gow. *Male Witches in Early Modern Europe*. Manchester, UK: Manchester University Press, 2003.

Bailey, Michael D. *Battling Demons: Witchcraft, Heresy, and Reform in the Late Middle Ages*. University Park: Pennsylvania State University Press, 2003.

Bartel, Pauline. *Spellcasters: Witches and Witchcraft in History, Folklore and Popular Culture*. Dallas, TX: Taylor, 2000.

Cavendish, Richard, ed. *Man, Myth, & Magic: The Illustrated Encyclopedia of Mythology, Religion, and the Unknown*. 21 vols. New York: Marshall Cavendish, 1995.

Clark, Stuart. *Thinking with Demons: The Idea of Witchcraft in Early Modern Europe*. New York: Oxford University Press, 1997.

Drury, Nevill. *Magic and Witchcraft: From Shamanism to the Technopagans*. New York: Thames & Hudson, 2003.

Frankfurter, David. *Evil Incarnate: Rumors of Demonic Conspiracy and Satanic Abuse in History*. Princeton, NJ: Princeton University Press, 2006.

Golden, Richard M., ed. *Encyclopedia of Witchcraft: The Western Tradition*. 4 vols. Santa Barbara, CA: ABC-CLIO, 2006.

Hill, Frances. *The Salem Witch Trials Reader*. New York: Da Capo, 2000.

Levack, Brian P. *The Witch-Hunt in Early Modern Europe*. 2nd ed. London: Longman, 1995.

Pickering, David. *Cassell Dictionary of Witchcraft*. London: Cassell, 1998.

Rabinovitch, Shelley. *The Encyclopedia of Modern Witchcraft and Neo-Paganism*. New York: Citadel, 2002.

Wicker, Christine. *Not in Kansas Anymore: A Curious Tale of How Magic Is Transforming America*. New York: HarperSanFrancisco, 2005.

Notes

Is It True?

Johannes Junius from Lara Apps and Andrew Gow, *Male Witches in Early Modern Europe* (Manchester, UK: Manchester University Press, 2003), 76–86, 159–166; Gardner quote from Gerald B. Gardner, *Witchcraft Today* (New York: Citadel, 2004), 29.

Chapter 1: A World of Witchcraft

Azande and Evans-Pritchard from Richard Cavendish, ed., *Man, Myth, & Magic: The Illustrated Encyclopedia of Mythology, Religion, and the Unknown,* vol. 20 (New York: Marshall Cavendish, 1995), 2815; Bantu familiars from Cavendish, vol. 20, 2828; Shakespeare's witches' recipe from *Macbeth*, Act IV, Scene 1, lines 1–38; Perkins quote from David Pickering, *Cassell Dictionary of Witchcraft* (London: Cassell, 1996), 85; Mesopotamian witchcraft and ritual from Walter Farber, "Witchcraft, Magic, and Divination in Ancient Mesopotamia," in Jack M. Sasson, ed., *Civilizations of the Ancient Near East*, vol. 3 (New York: Scribner's, 1995), 1989.

Chapter 2: The Hammer and the Hunt

Exodus quotation from King James Version; legal procedures from Brian P. Levack, "Witchcraft," in Paul F. Grendler, ed., *Encyclopedia of the Renaissance*, vol. 6 (New York: Scribner's, 1999), 313–314; chronology and geography of witch hunts from Levack, "Witchcraft," 314, and Cavendish, *Man, Myth, & Magic* vol. 6, 783–784; trial and execution figures from Levack, "Witchcraft," 314, and "Witchcraft" in Encyclopedia Britannica online at www.britannica.com/eb/article-214883/witchcraft; Pendle witch trials from Pickering, *Cassell Dictionary of Witchcraft*, 206–208; Demdike quote about image magic from Pickering, 141.

Chaper 3: Panic in America

"Evil hand" quote from John Hale, *A Modest Enquiry into the Nature of Witchcraft* (1702), quoted in Frances Hill, *The Salem Witch Trials Reader* (New York: Da Capo, 2000), 59; details of accusations and trials from Salem Witch Trials Documentary Archive and Transcription Project at jefferson.

village.virginia.edu/salem/further.html, and Hill, *The Salem Witch Trials Reader*, xix–xxii; Increase Mather sermon quote from Hill, xxii; Brattle quote from Hill, 98.

Chapter 4: Witches of the New Age
Crowley quotes, Lughnasadh ceremony, and chants from Vivianne Crowley, *The Magickal Life: A Wiccan Priestess Shares Her Secrets* (New York: Penguin, 2003), 264–266; number of Wiccans from Ontario Consultants on Religious Tolerance at www.religioustolerance.org/wic_nbr2.htm; "cats" quote from personal correspondence.

What Do You Think?
Salem as Witch Capital of the World from Christine Wicker, *Not in Kansas Anymore: A Curious Tale of How Magic Is Transforming America* (New York: Harper SanFrancisco, 2005), 12; Saudi Arabian execution from Amnesty International, "Death Penalty News, March 2000," at http://web.amnesty.org/library/Index/ENGACT530012000?open&of=ENG-BMU; India from G. Vijayam, "Investigating Witchcraft and Sorcery in Rangareddi District, India," *Skeptical Briefs*, June 2002, at www.csicop.org/sb/2002-06/india.html; Nigerian case from Leo Igwe, "Ritual Killing and Pseudoscience in Nigeria," *Skeptical Briefs*, June 2004, at www.csicop.org/sb/2004-06/nigeria.html; Zimbabwe law from Steve Vickers, "Witchcraft Ban Ends in Zimbabwe," BBC News, July 2, 2006, at news.bbc.co.uk/1/hi/world/africa/5134244.stm.

Index

Page numbers for illustrations are in boldface

About the Author

Rebecca Stefoff's many books for young readers cover a wide range of topics in science, history, and literature. Scary stories and vampire movies are among her favorite entertainments. As a member of CSICOP (the Committee for the Scientific Investigation of Claims of the Paranormal), Stefoff supports a thoughtful, research-based approach to supernatural and paranormal subjects. She lives in Portland, Oregon.